The discovery

'It's raining again,' said Amy.

It had been raining all week.

'If it doesn't stop raining soon,' said Dad, 'we'll be out of business. Nobody wants to come here in this terrible weather.'

Amy's parents owned a caravan site and a small grocery shop in the village.

It was a good place to spend a holiday.

But the last two summers had been very wet and few people wanted to stay in the caravans.

‘If things don’t get any better,’ said Mum, ‘we’ll have to sell the business and find some other work to do.’

‘We’ll have to move back to the town,’ said Dad.

‘But I don’t want to live in a town,’ said Amy.

Amy loved the country.
She liked the fields and trees and farm animals
but she didn't like the rain.
She went to help Dad clean one of the caravans.
Mrs Long, an archaeologist, was coming to stay in it.

‘What’s an archaeologist, Dad?’ asked Amy.

‘It’s somebody who is interested in history,’ explained Dad. ‘Mrs Long comes here every year. She looks for objects that have been buried in the ground for hundreds and hundreds of years.’

Mrs Long arrived after tea time.
Amy helped carry her things to the caravan.
'I'm sorry it's so wet,' said Amy. 'I hope it doesn't spoil your holiday.'
'Oh, I don't mind the rain,' said Mrs Long.

'Dad says you are going to look for things that have been lost,' said Amy. 'I hope you find what you are looking for.'

'I don't often find things,' laughed Mrs Long, 'but I keep on trying. One day I'll be lucky.'

Amy and Mrs Long went across the old wooden bridge into the fields on the other side of the river.

'That's where I shall be digging this week,' said Mrs Long. 'People have been living in this area for hundreds of years. It's a good place to dig.'

‘What are you hoping to find?’ asked Amy.

‘Anything that people might have lost or thrown away a long time ago,’ said Mrs Long. ‘Sometimes I find coins. Sometimes I find broken pots or toys.’

Amy said goodbye to Mrs Long and set off back to the caravan site to help Dad.

As she stepped on to the old wooden bridge it seemed to move under her feet.

'Be careful!' shouted Mrs Long. 'It's very slippery.'

Amy stepped back from the bridge quickly.
'The bridge doesn't look very safe,' said Mrs Long.

'I had better take you home the long way. The river is flooding and it looks as if the bridge might be swept away.'

Back at the caravan site Mum was getting worried.

'Where's Amy?' she asked.

'She's gone for a walk with Mrs Long,' said Dad.

'I hope they come back soon. I think there's going to be a storm.'

'I'll get the Landrover and fetch them both,' said Mum. 'They shouldn't be outside in this weather.'

Mum got into the Landrover and set off for the bridge.

It was raining so hard that she found it difficult to see where she was going.

Mum had just driven on to the bridge when she heard a shout.

She stopped and got out.

Mrs Long and Amy were waving to her from the far side.

'Go back!' they shouted. 'It's not safe.'

At that moment there was a terrific crack.

Mum jumped back from the bridge as the river began to flood over it.

'The Landrover!' cried Mum.

But there was nothing she could do.

The bridge began to break up.

Mum, Mrs Long and Amy all watched helplessly as the Landrover slid into the water.

It floated down the river and crashed into the bank.

Part of the river bank collapsed as the Landrover sank and stuck in the mud.

Mrs Long shouted to Mum.

'There's nothing you can do,' she called. 'Go back to the house and we'll go the long way round.'

A long time later Amy and Mrs Long arrived back at the house.

They were soaked, and shivering with cold.

They dried their hair and changed their clothes.

Dad made some hot drinks.

Mum and Dad were miserable.

'I don't know what we're going to do now,' said Dad. 'We can't afford a new Landrover and without it I can't collect the things we sell in the shop.'

'I think we'll just have to sell this caravan site,' said Mum, 'and move back to town.'

When Amy was in bed Mrs Long came into her room to say goodnight to her.

Amy was very upset.

'I don't want to move,' she said. 'I like living in the countryside and all my friends are here.'

'Don't worry,' said Mrs Long. 'I'm sure your Mum and Dad will think of something.'

'But if people don't stay in our caravans or buy things in our shop, we won't be able to stay,' said Amy.

The next day was really sunny.

'Well this makes a change,' said Mum. 'Perhaps we're going to have some fine weather now.'

'Does that mean we can stay?' asked Amy.

'We need more than good weather,' said Dad. 'We need lots of customers.'

'I'm going to see if I can find the Landrover,' said Mum. 'Or what's left of it. Do you want to come with me, Amy?'

Mum and Amy set off towards the river bank.

It was difficult to walk in the muddy fields.

The Landrover was still stuck in the mud.

'We'll have to get a tractor to pull it out,' said Mum. 'Then it can be sold for scrap.'

Amy began to explore the huge hole where the river bank had collapsed.

'Look at this Mum,' said Amy. 'There are lots of bits of coloured stone. Look at those jars stuck in the side of the bank.'

Mum seemed really excited.

'I'll get Mrs Long. This may be important,' she said.

Mrs Long was even more excited than Mum.
'Those coloured stones are called mosaics,' she said.
'I think you must have found a Roman Villa, Amy.'
'But look at those jars,' said Amy. 'What do you think is in them?'

'We'll soon see,' said Mrs Long.
She carefully lifted one of the jars.
'It's very heavy,' she gasped. 'I can hardly move it.'
'Let me help,' said Mum.

The jars were full of gold and silver coins.
'I can't believe my eyes!' gasped Mrs Long. 'What a fantastic find. I've been looking for this all my life.'
'Why is it important?' asked Amy.

'Archaeologists have searched for this Roman Villa for many years,' said Mrs Long. 'We knew it must be somewhere near here but none of us could find it. A few coins and bits of pottery were found but never the Villa itself.'

That afternoon people began to arrive in the village.
There were lots of archaeologists.
Newspaper reporters came as well.
Then the television cameras arrived.
By evening, Amy and her village were famous.

Hundreds of people came to the village to watch the archaeologists at work.

All the caravans were hired and Mum and Dad were busy all day in the shop.

'You won't have to move now,' laughed Mrs Long.

'Just think,' said Amy. 'If it wasn't for all that rain we would never have found the Roman Villa.'

'I told you things would work out,' said Mrs Long. 'It doesn't matter how hard it rains now. People will come to this village from all over the world.'

'Yes,' laughed Mum. 'To see my sunken Landrover!'

Printed in Hong Kong